THE NEW THEORY OF RELATIVITY

by Elijah Abramson, M.D.

Published by **crater era**

View and join our inclusive art house online at craterera.com

Connect with us on social media @craterera

Business and other inquiries can be directed to our email support at support@craterera.com

The New Theory of Relativity

APPLYING A CLASSICAL THEORY TO THE
PRESENT ERA

Elijah R. Abramson, M.D.

CRATER ERA || SAN FRANCISCO || 2025

PUBLISHED BY CRATER ERA

Copyright © 2025 by Elijah Abramson

All rights reserved. Published in the United States by crater era LLC, San Francisco, CA.

No part of this publication may be reproduced or transmitted in any form or by any means without the express written permission of the publishing company.

For information regarding permissions, please write to crater era at support@craterera.com. The company is based in northern California, specifically the San Francisco Bay Area.

https://www.craterera.com

ISBN: 9798284703830

First American edition, May 2025

In loving memory of

Isaiah Kyle Abramson

January 1995 -- September 2024

Should the form of the general equations some day, by the solution of the quantum problem, undergo a change however profound, even if there is a complete change in the parameters by means of which we represent the elementary process, the relativity principle will not be relinquished and the laws previously derived therefrom will at least retain their significance as limiting laws.

— Albert Einstein, July 1923

Contents

A. INTRODUCTION   1

B. ARTICLES

    ARTICLE I: **Paranoia** 3

    ARTICLE II: **Anger**   14

    ARTICLE III: **Anxiety** 23

    ARTICLE IV: **Sadness** 28

    ARTICLE V: **Finance**   32

C. CONCLUSION   34

INTRODUCTION

I believe that most legendary scientists were able to artistically apply their relative genius to special fields and subsequently develop theories that permanently altered the course of humanity. This includes people like Albert Einstein, Isaac Newton, and Leonardo da Vinci. Much of their thought was difficult for those not well versed in those fields to understand both in time and place in history. Complicated, lengthy, academic discussions can be challenging to apply to daily thought and conversation. However, I believe that these people, including Einstein, were effectively arguing philosophically and collegially amongst each other for how life should be lived.

I am going to single out Einstein's theory of relativity in this book because I think that while physically it makes sense, it can, in my opinion, be applied and understood more broadly. In today's age, intricate academic discussions are increasingly irrelevant to human health and happiness. Thus, an understanding of how relativity should apply to one's life is what I intend to introduce here. An understanding of what is emotionally relatively more or less important is, in my firmest opinion, critical to the health and happiness of humanity.

ARTICLE I: PARANOIA

Paranoia is one of the most destructive emotions. It is naturally impossible to quantify or rank emotions by harm. However, in my opinion, paranoia is the most toxic because if you develop a distortion of reality so potent that you are constantly watching your back then you are, by definition, not moving forward. While forward and backward are relative, this thought can be applied literally and figuratively.

A concrete example of this being applied literally is when you are walking down the street. If you are walking down a concrete sidewalk your eyes are always pointed in the same direction. Assume that you do not have mirrors or other objects produced by humanity. Whichever way you look, you cannot look 180 degrees to that direction. Thus the physical choice of the direction that you are pointed means you can not look in two opposing places at once. At any given moment, you must choose a direction. This is relatively intuitive.

More abstractly, emotionally, academically, or even professionally, you cannot look or study in two places at once. You have one physical body that can only be in one physical place at any given time therefore your attention must be on one thing at one time. If you are studying about basic sciences like reading a biology textbook then you are not studying linear algebra. If you are studying art history then you are not studying physics at that given time. Of course, there are nuances, but in general, it is physically impossible. Attention which has sometimes modernly been described as mindfulness is the understanding that you are doing one thing at one time. Therefore, it behooves of the individual to be happy with what they are doing at the present and understanding that that can and will change in the future. To be worried about what you are not doing while doing something else relatively important is to start to veer into paranoia. The intrusive concern of not doing what you are not doing can spiral and debilitate.

The most abstract application of an understanding of paranoia applies to thought itself. Humans think. Thought itself can be intrusive. But it can be highly difficult to understand whether a thought is paranoid. Not every word, sound, movement is perfect. Perfection as it is applied to human thought itself is an impossible ideal that will lead to an unhealthy desire to attain the unattainable.

As an example, schizophrenia generally requires auditory hallucinations. This means that you are hearing voices that are not there. In a sense, the idea is that you are responding to internal stimuli. However, hearing, voices, and internal stimuli can all be interpreted relatively or subjectively. Perception is reality and perception itself is relative.

As an example, one person who is relatively hard-of-hearing compared to another will hear a voice that is not there at any given decibel level. One person may be hard of hearing due to attending many loud concerts. Another person may be hard of hearing due to advancement in age. This is why one may see many babies and young children at concerts with earmuffs. When I was studying during medical school, I would often go to coffee shops with very powerful earmuffs so that way I could only "hear" what I was reading. The writing was not "talking" per se but perhaps I was reciting things in my head. I think any logical person who has ever read has essentially "talked to themselves in their head." Does that mean every person in the world has paranoia or schizophrenia because they have auditory hallucinations?

I believe that a logical person would agree beyond a reasonable doubt that the answer is no. And with advancement in age as well as certain acute or chronic medical conditions, one can be transiently or permanently "hard of hearing." But even those words, which are judged by medical professionals and utilized in medical documentation are relative. No healthcare professional has a decibel meter definition of hard of hearing. It is a ballpark estimate of how difficult it is to reasonably audibly communicate with the individual. Of course, there are also individuals with the born or acquired complete and permanent loss hearing. The sounds that they audibly make are different than those with the ability to communicate verbally in many cases. Does this mean that the internal stimuli that they are responding to visually is harmful or should be classified as paranoid? Certainly not.

I believe these examples prove that even the medical literature that defines "hearing voices that are not there" is relative. It is "subjectively" given by the patient to the physician who "objectively" assesses it and subsequently develops a plan. But patients are not subjects and physicians are not objects. Both humans are equally human. One just has the academic background to apply the thought understood by evidence-based scientific studies to their patients.

My stated belief in the previous paragraph could be easily and incorrectly misinterpreted. One could conclude that with this application of my new theory of relativity that medical literature and physician orders and plans are useless. This is ignorant. Western medicine has a troubled history, no doubt, but that, too, is a relative assessment itself. What should be taken from Western medicine is that its application has led to increased human life longevity. This, of course, says nothing about the quality of human lives, just that numerically the number of days or years has increased with correlation and causation secondary to evidence-based medicine or the application of scientific research to the human life (i.e. physical and metaphysical).

The application of the definition of paranoia is relative to other humans. If one becomes increasingly disconnected from reality (which is itself relative) then thoughts can spiral out of control. Many people and cultures believe that they "hear" voices of the past. But this is not literally true. It is metaphorically true meaning that an individual's memory of a voice is being "heard" in the present moment. In many cases, I would argue in most cases, this is good. This means that a person has learned from the past. The recollection of healthy life lessons applied to the present is good. For example, saying "I can hear Family Member A saying do not do this" when Person X is talking to Person Y can be quite productive if the "this" in that sentence is to harm oneself or someone else.

Here I would also like to provide relatively simple yet highly important examples of paranoid thoughts and choice. At a given time, paranoid or intrusive thoughts can be chosen or disregarded. That ability to delineate the two is good. Once you have lost the ability to choose whether or not to act or move forward with life in a paranoid state then you are veering into pathology.

Take, for example, an interaction with law enforcement. Very frequently, those with schizophrenia, psychosis, or other psychiatric illness develop relative obsession with conspiracy, distrust and paranoia toward law enforcement. If you are sitting in a coffee shop and a law enforcement officer walks in, you could think they are there to get you. In almost every case, that is not the case. They could be on a break getting coffee, nothing deeper than that. They could actually have good intentions and desire to get to know members and businesses in the community.

The vast majority of the time, this is their intention because they, like many adults, are performing a job and need breaks from that job. There is literally zero ill will from the perspective of the law enforcement officer despite the paranoid thought of the individual with that thought. Perhaps they disregard that intrusive thought and acknowledge its paranoid nature and possibly its connection to that individual's past trauma. The thought dissipates and life goes on. However, if they act on this paranoid thought, that could lead to trouble. If they cave to a primitive fight or flight response…that is when danger to self or others could possibly occur. Hopefully it does not, but it could. Danger to self or others is always bad.

Now, perhaps the danger that the individual feels only leads to a flight response. Perhaps their fear or anxiety related to the attire worn by the human in law enforcement in this scenario leads them to just leave the coffee shop prematurely. Perhaps they simply decide to finish their studies or work at home. No harm there, necessarily. But perhaps that individual continues to hone in on negative, paranoid thoughts whenever they see law enforcement personnel, paraphernalia, vehicles, etc. Now they find themselves in a mental space where no where outside is safe. They only feel safe within their home. Now an individual with a paranoid thought, effectively a delusional disorder, never leaves their home due to the perseverating concern that law enforcement is out to get them. Ideally, this individual could flip their thinking into believing perhaps law enforcement is out to help them, the exact opposite of their paranoid thought. Then maybe they could entertain the idea of exposure therapy in the real world, in a sense. Perhaps the law enforcement officer walks in and the individual says "hello" and starts a brief conversation with the officer. Now the officer gets to know a member of the community, appreciates the acknowledgement, and the paranoid individual can possibly realize the irrational nature of their thought and realize they have made a step to overcome it. This is productive.

That being said, there are many examples where paranoid thought can spiral. Command hallucinations are defined as auditory hallucinations where an individual (i.e. a patient) is instructed to act in specific ways. Well then does not the very example I discussed above with hearing voices of the past qualify as an auditory hallucination? I would argue yes, again proving the relativity of a command hallucination. The application by medical professionals with this thought insofar as it requires physical or chemical modification is when that command causes harm. Harm can be to the individual or to others. A classic example would be an individual with mental (i.e. psychiatric) illness who has a thought commanding them to do harm to themselves or others. While this is a relatively general statement, I think many adults have seen or heard or read examples of what this harm can be.

In reality, it is not the structure of the thought that is harmful. It is the functional distortion that it causes.

Thus, the physician is applying their thought of relative harm to the patient's thoughts. The physician is quite literally the judge of thought in this scenario. That is tremendous power. A good mental health professional respects the application of this power. A good patient respects the application of this power, as well.

However, even *the setting itself* of the judge of thought (the mental health professional) and the patient is relative. The power is granted to the physician only in the setting of a healthcare office or hospital. In the community or "in the street," that power dynamic is relatively irrelevant. If a physician and a patient interact in the street, there is no authority for the physician to command a patient to follow certain orders or a plan. It may be wise to do so, but there is no obligation to sit down for a specified duration of time to deconstruct paranoid thoughts and construct a good plan to move forward. In fact, the role of physician and patient is arbitrary because every licensed physician in the United States born in a hospital was a patient at one time. So basically every physician was or is also a patient.

Even more abstractly, the relative roles are impossible to determine without a badge or certification. For example, if a psychiatrist and a mentally ill patient are both yelling at each other in the street, it would be impossible to tell which person is the psychiatrist and which person is the mentally ill patient if both were wearing plainclothes unless you knew the roles of both individuals. All you would see is two people yelling at each other. Especially if you were not relatively close enough to hear and assess the words for yourself, all you would see is two people yelling. A reasonable person could certainly determine that both people are mentally ill.

Thus, I believe paranoid thought is at its core most aptly described as a breakdown in trust. It is a loss of trust of oneself in oneself and/or a loss of trust of oneself in others. And we are at a time and age where there is such a catastrophic loss of trust. There is an inability to distinguish what decisions are binary and what decisions are on a spectrum. From a patient's perspective, not every physician is "good" and not every physician is "bad." But at a certain point, you must trust someone. You must choose to trust at least one physician. That is essentially an example where trust is binary. If a patient decides that this decision is not binary, then they will seek a second opinion. Then a third opinion. Then a fourth opinion. When does that spectrum stop? It may not.

I have personally witnessed patients that do this. Those impatient patients will, if ever, receive good healthcare. They will likely blame their poor health on the healthcare system when in reality it is largely their own doing. Continuity of care is critical to health because there are very few specialties like my medical specialty, emergency medicine, where a patient-physician interaction must be brief and may never occur again.

Particularly with regards to outpatient mental health services, continuity of care is critical that way a physician and patient can develop that trust to where the physician's expertise is applied over relative time. If the function of the patient relatively improves day-to-day or month-to-month, then that is a highly valuable relationship. That patient may only need one psychiatrist for their life.

At a certain point, a patient must trust that their physician is good enough. This, of course, can and should be applied more broadly than to just psychiatric medical care. But, I would caution, to strictly assume that physicians are the gatekeepers toward any individual's mental health is inaccurate. The functional assessment of mental health is happiness. It is are you interacting with society in such a way where you are performing basic life functions like eating, sleeping, playing, and working.

We do not always (and ideally would rarely, if ever) need a physician to make this assessment for us. A soliloquy can be just as beautiful as a monologue but if you cannot distinguish between the two, therein lies the problem.

ARTICLE II: ANGER

Anger itself is also relative. This is where words and thoughts matter. For the sake of this argument, I will make a distinction between anger and rage. Anger is a negative emotion where you develop a relatively negative feeling toward someone or something else. Despite this being defined as a negative, it is a positive. What I mean by this is that anger is good insofar as it is a natural recognition that something is being done that needs to be responded to in a certain way. This response is, without deeper thought, essentially either fight or flight.

If someone says or does something offensive to you, that will make you angry. But that offensive thing is relative, as is the defensive response. In medicine and in law and in general, the response can be proportional or disproportional. If someone says they are going to hurt you, that would make a rational person angry. If they do physically or emotionally hurt you, then it is certainly reasonable to be angry. But if you respond in this 'example A' to a threat of violence with physical violence that causes tremendous physical harm, then you are not responding proportionally. I think the most harmless display in reaction to an initial threat is actually a retaliatory threat of physical harm. Even the passive aggressive escalation of threat of violence can develop into an emotional cold war which could lead to real physical violence. However, if you respond with this 'example B' by asking the person to not cause the physical harm (i.e. verbal de-escalation) then that justified anger, even if the decibel level of the voice in which it is projected in is relatively louder than the initial comment, is quite a reasonable response.

For this argument, I will classify the first example in the previous paragraph as rage. The second example in the above, which is appropriate, is anger. Thus, anger is a positive-negative emotion. Rage is a negative-negative emotion. Mathematically, this does not compute because a negative multiplied by a positive is a negative and a negative multiplied by a negative is a positive. Due to that contrast, I think that this is a sort of proof that emotional computation is not similar to mathematical computation. Some negative emotions are positive. Some negative emotions are negative. Understanding the difference between the two is critical to health regardless of the name applied to the emotion.

I think even in classifying emotional response to anger- and rage-causing incidents, we should distinguish between what I will characterize as "reactions" and "responses."

Reactions are instantaneous, often poorly thought out, words and actions relative to the initial incitement. Responses are, for the sake of this argument, more deliberate and well-thought out words and actions relative to the initial incitement.

Certainly some anger- and rage-provoking incidents will require relatively quick responses that could appear as reactions. For example, if someone brandishes a knife in front of you, your reaction or response is based on your ability to perceive that threat.

The best response in that scenario would be "flight." The reason that this response or reaction is the best is because it is the one that causes you no harm and the inciting person no harm. Doing no harm is good.

There could be situations where this response is impossible. One example would be if you are in an enclosed, small space (i.e. a locked room). If that is the case, you essentially have no decision but to fight. In that scenario, if you do not fight, you will be subject to physical harm. That is not good. Harm reduction is always good.

All of this being said, there is another scenario or outcome that I alluded to but have not yet discussed. This is one of a response of self-reflection. If you are in a setting where you are having a discussion and a comment makes you angry, then your best response may be to listen and reflect.

For example, if someone says that you are angry and that makes you more angry, then perhaps you are angry. Perhaps, in fact, you have rage. In that case, your best response may be to listen and consider why you are angry. If someone says that you are underperforming and that makes you angry, then it may be good to simply consider why that made you angry. Sometimes, the truth can make you angry. That does not mean that it is not the truth.

For example, if an examiner states an examinee underperformed (i.e. did not pass) an examination, then anger may be the truthful emotion the examinee feels. It may, however, better be perceived as an opportunity for improvement or redirection. A healthy self-reflection, instead of anger or rage directed at the examiner or exam itself, could be either: a) what do I need to do to retake or pass this examination or b) should I pursue a different direction? There may be more than two options in the self reflection of the perceived failure or underperformance in the examination, however it is true that anger directed at the examiner or examination does nothing productive for the examinee. This anger or rage is counterproductive to the health and life of the examinee in this scenario.

Another example of anger or rage could be in relationship to a technological or wifi malfunction. If your music player briefly skips a beat or your internet connection transiently stops working, that could make you angry. Aside from it being sad that this makes you angry, you could act on this thought in two relatively opposing ways. In an extreme scenario, you could break your computer. You could violently blame the technology itself. You could call up the internet service provider and yell at a customer service representative that the internet is out. In many cases, that is absolutely a waste of time and energy.

Alternatively, you could respond to that "malfunction" with a reflective thought that it could be a sign to get off of the internet and interact with the real world. Perhaps you are going down a rabbit hole that is a poor use of time and energy. Maybe instead, you should go for a walk, run, bicycle ride, etc.

To me, the latter is clearly a much better approach to a technological malfunction. Now of course, this is not a fully binary choice. If you have internet that works 99 percent of the time, it goes out, and comes back an hour or so later, then that is not a problem. But if the internet works 99 percent of the time and all of a sudden it is not working for hours that become days, for example, then of course, yes, logically you need to address that head on. But to be unable to distinguish the need for two different responses in those two different scenarios is problematic.

Of course, the majority of life is not a literal examination. It should not be perceived as such, in my opinion. If you are perceiving your entire life, or even the majority of your life, as a formal or literal examination then you have, by definition, placed your life in someone else's hands. You are subjecting your existence to that of someone else.

While I firmly believe in the value of K-12 education and higher education, if you continue to spend your life pursuing degrees and passing examinations, I would argue you are not living a happy life. You are simply continually subjecting yourself to someone else's opinion that you have misclassified as objective. Childhood and adulthood education is important but all "formal" education should have its limits. Otherwise there would be no professors at scholastic institutions, there would only be students. At a certain point in life, you have to decide I am either a) ready to become a professor or b) ready to exit the formal educational process as a student. Enter your profession or source of employment, contribute to society, and remain a lifelong learner outside of the halls of an institution.

On this note, some people may be angered or offended simply by questions. For example, someone could ask you: why are you pursuing a fellowship? If that simple question produces an emotional response of anger or rage, then it may show up in the verbal reaction.

An example of an angry reaction would be answering that question with a question. For example, asking why the asker wants to know. The reason responding to that question with a question is an example of an angry response is because it attempting to manipulate or redirect the conversation. The likely intent is arrogance and/or ignorance. It could be the assumption that the person asking the question has ill will. It could be the arrogant feeling that the person asking the question is unintelligent or less intelligent and therefore does not even deserve a response. It could be avoidant because you may not have truly considered why you are doing it. It could be because you do not know why you are doing or saying it.

Thus, the angry response is inappropriate and counterproductive to both the conversation as well as the individual offended by the initial question. It could have been a great opportunity to self reflect on intentions but is instead perceived as antagonism. There are many other examples like this. I think by and large answering questions with questions is based in anger, rage, avoidance and/or arrogance. This is unless the second question is genuinely asking for clarification of the original one.

For example, if the person being asked the question is actually undertaking two fellowships, a reasonable clarifying question would be: which fellowship are you talking about or are you asking about both? That is a very reasonable clarifying question. That is in no way based in anger, rage, or antagonism. In general, asking questions is good. But here you can see an example where it may not be so good.

Abstractly, the initial ask of "why" is good. It creates an opportunity to self-reflect and/or share with another individual about themselves. The second ask of "why" may or may not be good in the sense of continuing productive dialogue. It is based in counterproductive emotions and will likely redirect the conversation. It, quite likely, could escalate an innocuous and genuine question into a verbal altercation if a(n) individual(s) in that conversation are confrontational. If they are avoidant (i.e. avoidant personality disorder), then they may simply shut down and the conversation may end.

While the adage that there are no dumb questions may be true, there are certainly questions that are relatively better than other ones. Ones that are not so good will devolve a conversation into more counterproductive negative emotions.

I think it is good to do your best to avoid asking questions that devolve a conversation into a confrontation and avoid allowing a question to offend you. At a certain point, yes, every conversation will end, in a sense, but doing your best to be sure that questions and responses are well intended is the best way to be. Perhaps you have identified a person that is at their core quite arrogant. Then yes, perhaps avoiding that person altogether is best both for you and for them. But on the other hand, if a good person asks a good question and your reaction is to shut down or ask a non-clarifying question…well, perhaps you should consider why your emotional response is a negative one.

ARTICLE III: ANXIETY

Anxiousness can be good or bad. For simpleness, the disorders in the psychiatric literature described as social and generalized anxiety disorders are bad. Why are they bad? Well, again, this is simply because they are identification that the structure of the thought of the patient has led to a functional decline. This is intuitive because anxiety in social situations can lead to debilitating fear of entering into any social situation.

This could theoretically lead to complete isolationism where the individual does not leave whatever they have classified as their home. Especially in America today, if someone has a smartphone, they could theoretically be the owner-occupant of real estate like a condominium or single-family home and never leave the home.

If they have the financial resources, they could auto-pay all bills, order food delivery from their phone, watch television on their phone, play video games on their phone, and spend time on social media on their phone. This theoretically relatively anxious person would be so debilitated that they literally may never set foot outside of their "home." That, in my opinion, is sad. That is a person who needs rehabilitation. That is what the real community, real family, real friends, and professional services should help with. Certainly, that person will not magically become a paragon of integration into society but ideally the anxiousness in social situations will slowly subside with assistance to the point where they develop more healthy interactions with their community.

Generalized anxiety is, of course, more difficult to provide concrete examples for because it is generalized and not specific to social situations. Relatively speaking, it is anxiousness in multiple settings that leads to functional impairment.

Without getting too far into the medical and psychiatric jargon and literature, this means that an individual is unable to perform basic life functions due to irrational worry or fear (i.e. the very definition of anxiety). Just like any emotions, there may be one or multiple very valid reasons a person has this irrational anxiety but the validity or perseverance on its validity is itself irrational. It is counterproductive.

Sure, an anxious person can obsessively reiterate or justify their actions as being due to anxiety but that does them no good. It is immaturely focusing on a word or a part of their past and justifying current or future actions because of the past.

This could be you just sadly continuing generational or childhood trauma. And if this energy is passed down, then you are regenerating generational trauma yourself. That is not good. Programs for substance misuse often identify recognition as a first step in improvement. They do not say that the improvement starts and stops with perseverating on recognition of your shortcomings. It is the first step in a process to minimize the impact of a past problem on your current and future life. That is how you are an agent for change and reduction of generational trauma. Sometimes family, friends, the community, and lifestyle changes are enough to manage anxiety. In this case, it is not pathologic. It is normal. But if you, in concert with these people, struggle to manage the anxiousness, then yes, of course, seeking and taking the advice from medical professionals is a good idea.

Thus, anxiety absolutely exists on a spectrum. This is true both socially and generally. What is nuanced and so difficult is that it is the training of medical professionals to effectively map or assess what on the spectrum does not require behavioral or medical modification and what does require those modifications.

If we decide that physicians, and particularly psychiatrists, are the gatekeepers for assessment and management of anxiety then every single person needs a psychiatrist. And that would mean every psychiatrist needs a psychiatrist. Then there would be no possibility for the vast majority of people to see a psychiatrist. But we have arrived at a time in history where people so quickly jump to telling other people "you should see a psychiatrist" or "you should see a therapist" with no reasonable justification.

Now our systems are overwhelmed and increasingly under-qualified to provide care to those who need it. Thus, again, we return to the fundamental truth of self-reflection of living a happy and healthy life. Much of primary care recommendations require "lifestyle modifications." If you are able to modify your lifestyle in such a way that you only require annual or semiannual maintenance appointments and preventative testing, then that is ideal. That is a system not stressed to its limits. That is a trained, evidence-based system that is providing a valuable service.

Has any anxious person who over-identifies with their academic degrees and other titles and never leaves their house living a life as fulfilling, meaningful, and happy as another person half their biological age who has relatively fewer degrees, titles but travels regularly and lives and contributes as they wish happily in their community? I hope that is a rhetorical question. If the truth causes anxiety, that is ok. Put in the work to reduce the anxiety if it is causing functional impairment in your own mind or in the opinion of those that genuinely love and care about you.

ARTICLE IV: SADNESS

Sadness is probably the most difficult emotion to characterize in terms of health. Relatively speaking, it is extremely common. It is extremely normal. Anger turning into rage is clearly toxic and possibly easiest to identify based on tone of voice, tenor of conversation, and other things. Sadness is difficult to determine because I definitely think that the spectrum from happy to sad is so far from binary that it is almost entirely grey except at the extreme ends. If one were to visualize this emotional spectrum as a normal distribution, this curve is very flat as opposed to bell-shaped. If that is the case, then how does one tell what is pathological depression versus normal sadness?

I think applying a stoic philosophy to emotion is critical to being able to maintain normal emotional stability and lability. To "perfect" happiness or sadness is effectively to become a robot. There is no seesaw-style perfect balance that can or should be maintained throughout human life. That is effectively the complete elimination of human emotion. This is why materialism as a school of thought or philosophy is invalid.

A relative amount of happiness and sadness throughout the day and week and month, etcetera is normal. I would argue that happy individuals are just able to maneuver out of sadder states more adeptly and frequently. To reiterate something that I have said, it is not the structure of the emotions that you should psychoanalyze with great depth. It is the function that matters more. If the amount of happiness and sadness that you experience is relatively stable and your interactions with others is also fairly stable, then that is something that really does not need to be actively focused on with great detail. Self-reflection takes time and energy too, so it is important to live your life with happiness, peace, and purpose. But if your sadness is leading to depression, then that is something that needs to be addressed.

The issue is of course where does the relative amount of sadness that you experience veer into pathological major depression disorder? Well, number one, I think depression is so prevalent and culturally misunderstood by laypeople that the focus or use of these words has really lost meaning. The healthcare professionals who are dedicated to effective assessment of this are both academically trained and clinically experienced with determining the difference. Thus, relative trust is again critical.

You have to sit down and find a professional who you trust enough to have longitudinal conversations with because emotions cannot realistically be instantaneously assessed, diagnosed, and permanently fixed. The factors in this assessment including sadness, appetite loss, sleep loss, anhedonia, psychomotor disturbances are all spectral in nature. But, I have found those who enter the mental healthcare system are so determined to overanalyze their unique psyche that they do not accept that their diagnosis is actually quite common. I find this to be sad because if you understand the relatively common nature of your condition and can see those around you who have overcome it, then you can empower yourself by the simple thought connection that knowing someone else did it so you can, too. Instead, people like that tend to jump down rabbit holes of despair which will naturally lead to further isolation and pathological sadness (i.e. depression).

It is for this reason that I think an understanding of sadness is particularly critical. It is so normal and yet with social media, artificial intelligence, pandemics, and other incredibly isolating surroundings in this era it can and has gotten incredibly out of hand. It starts with being withdrawn from professional and personal environments. It progresses to incredible dependence on either "recreational" substances or technology. It ultimately ends with severe physical and mental isolation. And at its worst, of course, the primary normal emotion of sadness can theoretically progress to suicide which is, again, the complete loss of the physical and emotional self.

In fact, I think relatively uncontrolled sadness is often the primary cause that leads to uncontrolled anger, anxiety, and paranoia. Next, and finally, I will discuss how the emotional reality connects with the modern intermediary to the physical world.

ARTICLE V: FINANCE

Money is obviously relative. This is proven by the fact that currency from country to country varies in value. Centuries ago, money did not exist. Goods and services were simply traded for goods and services. Money is literally the intermediary. And yet there are so many people that overvalue the intermediary that in isolation literally holds no value. It may be paper. It may be metal. It may be cryptically computed on the world wide web also known as the internet. And even the so-called single number that describes one's financial wealth, net worth, changes relative to time.

The value of currency changes second to second. The value in which the money is invested—i.e. stocks, mutual funds, real estate—changes equally as quickly.

Yet sadly, many people decide on pursuing a profession or relationship with an individual based on money a.k.a. an intermediary that changes by the second. That is both sad and illogical.

An individual that does that is lost.

They have decided to make the means the end when the means could theoretically be, and historically was, nonexistent. They have literally placed a price on a human and that human is themselves. There is no price on time or humanity because price itself is arbitrary. Human emotion, life, relationships, community, health and happiness are priceless. There are many examples of communities and individuals with less financial means that have better relationships, closer communities, better health, and more happiness than those with more financial means.

Thus, I believe one should never fixate on money itself. And if you have identified an individual clearly fixated on money itself, then that is a person to avoid spending a relatively large amount of time with considering your time is priceless and they have solely identified their time as it relates to money.

CONCLUSION

Time is priceless. Happiness is priceless.

Be careful with paranoia, anger, rage, anxiety, sadness, and fixation on an intermediary like money. Self-reflect, utilize and participate in your community. The present is a present, treat it and live in it as such. Spend it learning, playing, teaching, and having fun.

If you have forgotten what is fun for you, think what made you happy as a child and do that. Do what you can to be optimistic and realistic.

A positive attitude must not be dimmed by a negative attitude or negative people. A negative attitude should be addressed, supported, and hopefully improved.

Happiness is a relative state that will be best achieved most regularly if you can (among other things) minimize the influence of paranoia, rage, anxiety, sadness, and fixation on money.

These concepts, to me, are the building blocks of how we can, in a sense, apply Einstein's Theory of Relativity in a new way to human emotion and the current human experience. If you spend too much time with the negative emotions discussed in these articles, then you have lost a sense of what is relatively more important and what is relatively less important. If you do that, then you are on track to lose yourself.

Elijah Abramson, M.D. is an artist and scientist who is also a board-certified American physician specializing in all emergencies, currently practicing in the state of California. His wide-ranging personal and professional life experiences continue to expand his knowledge base as well as desire to share it. He has lived and worked in (as well as travelled to) a variety of under-resourced communities. He hopes to share his art through multiple mediums to bring light where there is or was darkness. He lives in Sacramento, CA.

Made in the USA
Middletown, DE
18 June 2025